5 LEAD GENERATION STRATEGIES FOR SMALL BUSINESSES

How to Build a Bulletproof Prospects Base and 10x Your Sales with Lowest Cost

Princewill Ukpabio

COPYRIGHT

Copyright © 2024 www.ukdigitalworld.com All rights reserved.

No part of this publication may be reproduced, distributed, or transmitted in any form or by any means, including photocopying, recording, or other electronic or mechanical methods, without the prior written permission of the publisher, except in the case of brief quotations embodied in critical reviews and certain other noncommercial uses permitted by copyright law.

For permissions requests, contact the publisher at nobleprinceukpabio@gmail.com.

The information provided in this book is for general informational purposes only. While every effort has been made to ensure the accuracy and completeness of the information, the author and publisher assume no responsibility for errors or omissions, or for damages resulting from the use of the information contained herein.

Trademarks mentioned in this book are the property of their respective owners. The use of trademarks is solely for identification purposes and does not imply any affiliation with or endorsement by the trademark owners.

Some of the links in the eBook are affiliate links. You will get a discounted price if you purchase through those type of links, and I may get a little commission from it.

ABOUT THE BOOK

This book presents a comprehensive guide to proven 5 lead generation tactics, drawing inspiration from the strategies implemented by industry giants such as Rolex, Apple, Tesla, and others. This book is a valuable resource for small businesses seeking to elevate their lead generation efforts and achieve substantial growth.

Through this book, readers will gain insights into five meticulously tested and proven lead generation strategies that have yielded exceptional results for renowned companies. By distilling these strategies into actionable steps, Princewill Ukpabio empowers small business owners and entrepreneurs to harness the same principles and techniques to propel their enterprises forward.

Emphasizing the potential for transformative impact, this book advocates for the adoption of these strategies by small businesses, highlighting the potential for substantial turnaround and sustained success. With a clear focus on practical application and real-world relevance, this book equips readers with the tools and knowledge needed to leverage cutting-edge lead generation tactics in a manner tailored to the unique needs and challenges of small businesses.

By distilling the success stories of global industry leaders into actionable insights, this book serves as a compelling manifesto for small businesses, offering a roadmap to unlock their full potential and achieve remarkable growth. "**5 Lead Generation Strategies for Small Businesses**" is a testament to the transformative power of strategic lead generation and its capacity to revolutionize the trajectory of small businesses, making it an indispensable resource for entrepreneurs and business owners alike.

ABOUT THE AUTHOR

Princewill Ukpabio is a seasoned IT specialist and Digital Marketer with a Higher National Diploma (HND) in Computer Science. His passion is to empower small businesses to thrive in the digital economy. With over five years of experience in digital marketing, He has dedicated himself to helping businesses generate leads and maximize their online presence.

Driven by his love for small businesses, He was inspired to write this book to share his tested strategies for business growth and lead generation. His expertise in digital marketing has not only been honed through years of professional experience, but also through the successful implementation of the very strategies discussed in this book, both in his own business and with his clients. The glowing testimonies from these experiences are a testament to the effectiveness of his methods.

Apart from this book, Princewill has authored a book on Search Engine Optimization, "**Mastering SEO in The Age of AI**". His commitment to staying at the forefront of digital marketing trends and strategies is evident in his hobbies, which revolve around continuous learning and discovering new ways to enhance businesses, both his own and those of his clients.

If you wish to connect with him, you can visit his website at https://www.ukdigitalworld.com or find him on LinkedIn as **"Princewill Ukpabio"**, where He will continue to share more visibility, and business insights and engage with you more.

TABLE OF CONTENT

COPYRIGHT 2

ABOUT THE BOOK 4

ABOUT THE AUTHOR 6

TABLE OF CONTENT 8

INTRODUCTION 11

    What is a lead? 12

    Why Do People Want to Buy? 15

ONLINE SELF-ASSESSMENT 19

WAITLIST 23

    Benefits of a Waitlist Strategy 23

    How to Implement a Waitlist Strategy with ScoreApp
.... 24

    Successful Companies Using Waitlist Strategy 26

ONLINE DISCUSSION GROUPS 30
  Why Use Online Discussion Groups? 30
  How to Maximize the Potential of Online Discussion Groups 31
WORKSHOPS/SEMINARS 35
  Benefits of Small Workshops/Seminars 35
  Step-by-Step Guide on How to Effectively Invite Your B2B Prospects 36
    Step 1: Identify Your Target Audience 36
    Step 2: Create a Compelling Invitation 36
    Step 3: Personalize Your Invitations 37
    Step 4: Utilize Multiple Channels 37
    Step 5: Provide Clear Details 38
    Step 6: Follow-Up 38
    Step 7: Offer Incentives 38
    Step 8: Track and Analyze Responses 38
  Maximizing the Impact of Your Workshops/Seminars 39
PRIVATE DINNER 41
  Key Elements of a Successful Private Dinner Event . 43
  Enhancing the Private Dinner Experience 44
    Personalized Invitations 44
    Themed Discussions 45

SUMMARY 48
RECOMMENDATIONS... 50

INTRODUCTION

The reason most small businesses remain small is not because they have the wrong business model, product, or services, but it's because they can't make enough sales and generate more revenue to be considered a large business. Some may be because of laziness to act fast and do what must be done and at the right time.

Here's the problem, most businesses are too comfortable where they at that they think that's their ceiling. Most small businesses make around 5 figures per month and feel like they can't grow beyond that. But I'm here to challenge you that if you implement the 5 lead generation strategies I've discussed in this book, you'll make more than you could ever imagine.

These are the five strategies that the big companies use, and they don't reveal to you so you can't try to compete with them or outgrow their revenue. It's like in the financial industry, the fewer people that speak the financial jargon the more money they make, and the more money they charge for not understanding how the financial games are played.

What is a lead?

To keep it simple and short, a lead is a signal of interest. This is an individual or organization that has shown interest in your products or services and has the potential to become a future customer. This interest can be expressed through various actions, such as visiting your website, signing up for a newsletter, or downloading content.

There are several types of leads based on their engagement and readiness to purchase:

- **Marketing Qualified Leads (MQLs):** These leads have shown interest in your marketing efforts and are more likely to become customers than other types of leads. They might have filled out a form, downloaded a whitepaper, or attended a webinar.
- **Sales Qualified Leads (SQLs):** These are leads that have been evaluated by the sales

team as ready for a direct sales follow-up. They have indicated a clear intent to purchase your product or service.
- **Product Qualified Leads (PQLs):** These are individuals who have used your product (often through a free trial or freemium model) and have shown interest in becoming a paying customer.
- **Service Qualified Leads (SRLs):** These are leads that have indicated they are interested in your services, possibly by directly contacting your service team.

Understanding these types can help tailor your approach to convert them into paying customers effectively.

People don't buy because of how great your product is, or how well-established you think you are. They buy for their reasons, not yours. So, if you can make them see the value that your product will bring to them, and how much faster it will take them to get what they want from using your product, or accepting the service you render, the more likely it is there for them to want to buy.

But you can't just explain how great your product is, or be a pushy salesperson, pressuring them, to make them want to say yes to what you want to sell to them. This is not a sales book, but you must understand the connection on what makes people want to buy anything.

It's not about setting huge marketing budgets. It's about the little things that matter most to your prospects. How do you know what is in their mind, and how do you pitch them the solution you can offer to solve that problem easier, more effectively, and more efficiently for them.

You can have 10 million dollars of advertising budget and get as many sales as the "vague advertising" can generate, but you are losing in the game. Do you know what you have done instead? You are running in a rabbit hole and potentially making the advertising agency or company richer while you remain at your ceiling level and will never break through and see behind the curtain.

The bottom line is this: If you're a small business no matter how good your product is, but you can't generate leads, you don't have a business. On the flip side, if Cristiano Ronaldo, with his massive followership which he could potentially turn into leads, would enter your industry and have a very basic product that is not as good as your product, he would probably make a billion dollars.

So, everything in business is downstream to lead generation. If you don't have a lead, you don't have a business. In Economics, there's what it's called "**supply and demand tension**." If you have thousands and potentially millions of leads and have a limited product, then it will create tension. People will fight over your product because they know there are thousands of others waiting to buy if they miss the opportunity to buy immediately. That's the power of being oversubscribed.

Why Do People Want to Buy?

Understanding the psychological factors that influence buying decisions can be crucial for effective lead generation. Here's why people make purchasing decision:

1. **Emotional Influence:** People often make purchases based on emotions rather than logic. A product or service that evokes positive feelings, like happiness or excitement, is more likely to be purchased.
2. **Social Proof:** Potential customers look to others for reassurance before making a purchase. Testimonials, reviews, and recommendations from friends can significantly impact buying decisions.
3. **Authority:** Buyers are influenced by experts or authoritative figures. If a respected figure endorses a product, it can increase trust and likelihood of purchase.
4. **Scarcity and Urgency:** The perception that a product is scarce, or an offer is time-limited can create a sense of urgency, prompting quicker buying decisions.
5. **Value Perception:** The perceived value of a product, which includes quality, benefits, and cost, plays a pivotal role in decision-making. A higher perceived value can justify a higher price point.

6. **Mental Shortcuts:** Consumers often use heuristics or mental shortcuts to make quick decisions. For example, a higher price might be equated with higher quality.
7. **The Power of Free:** The idea of getting something for free is highly attractive and can drive people to make purchases to obtain the free item or service.

Small businesses, while they may lack the long-standing reputation of larger companies, can still effectively generate warm leads by leveraging their unique strengths and adopting smart strategies.

Personalization is key; small businesses can offer tailored experiences that larger businesses often cannot match. Engaging directly with customers through personalized communication and customer service can create a memorable brand experience.

Community involvement also plays a significant role. Being active in local events and online communities can help small businesses build relationships and increase visibility within their target market. Content marketing is another powerful tool; by providing valuable and informative content, small businesses can establish authority and trust in their niche.

Referral programs can incentivize existing customers to spread the word, effectively turning them into brand ambassadors. Also, small businesses should focus on optimizing their online presence, ensuring their website is user-friendly and their social media profiles are active and engaging.

So, if you are a small business that is struggling to get qualified leads, or increasing your leads, make sure you go through this book thoroughly. If possible, get a pen and jotter to jot down some important strategies you will get from this book in your words for better understanding. This will also help you when going through it the next time. Without wasting time, let's start with the first lead generation strategy on our list.

ONLINE SELF-ASSESSMENT

Our first strategy for lead generation is Online self-assessment, this is a powerful strategy. It involves creating a digital tool or questionnaire that allows prospects to evaluate if they are a good fit for the product you want to sell to them. This self-assessment tool is typically hosted on a website or landing page, where users can access and answer a series of questions.

One of the main advantages of online self-assessment is its ability to capture valuable information about potential leads. By engaging users in a self-assessment process, you can gather data on their interests, needs, and pain points. This information can then be used to tailor your marketing and sales efforts, ensuring that you offer relevant solutions to your audience.

Let's say your product is for people who want to lose weight. If you did an online self-assessment for people who want to lose weight. And your product focuses on exercise, and workouts. If you set up a strategic online self-assessment, you can find out what else your prospect would want instead of your core product. They may need other things like recipes, or nutrition plans to be in good shape.

To effectively use online self-assessment as a lead generation tool, it is essential to design the questionnaire in a way that provides value to the user. The questions should be thought-provoking, insightful, and relevant to their needs. By offering valuable insights and actionable recommendations based on their responses, you can establish yourself as an authority in your field and build trust with your audience.

To create an online self-assessment that generates leads. You must provide a high-quality user experience and use persuasive copywriting techniques to engage users and encourage them to complete the assessment.

One tool that can greatly enhance the effectiveness of your online self-assessment is **ScoreApp**. This is a powerful platform that allows you to create interactive and engaging self-assessment experiences. With ScoreApp, you can easily design and customize your assessment questions, track user responses, and generate detailed reports.

Additionally, ScoreApp offers features such as lead capture and integration with customer relationship management (CRM) systems, enabling you to seamlessly manage and nurture your leads.

ScoreApp AI can help you create a better online self-assessment if you are new to creating an online assessment. You can enhance the user experience, gather valuable data on your leads, and streamline your lead generation and nurturing processes. With its robust features and intuitive interface, ScoreApp is a recommended tool for maximizing the effectiveness of your online self-assessment strategy.

Instead of selling your core product at first, you sell them an online assessment to determine if they are a good fit for the product, or if there is a better product you could sell to them to solve their problem. Online self-assessment is an efficient way to generate leads.

By creating a valuable and engaging self-assessment tool, you can capture valuable data on your audience, establish yourself as an authority, and tailor your marketing efforts to their specific needs. **ScoreApp** is a recommended tool to create a better online self-assessment, offering features that enhance the user experience and streamline lead management processes.

WAITLIST

A waitlist is a powerful lead generation strategy that can help your business generate interest, build anticipation, and create a sense of exclusivity around your products or services. Using the concept of scarcity and creating a sense of urgency, a waitlist can effectively generate leads and convert them into customers. This is about creating demand and scarcity to attract customers and build a thriving business.

Benefits of a Waitlist Strategy

1. **Creating anticipation:** By offering limited availability and exclusivity, a waitlist strategy can generate excitement and anticipation among potential customers. This anticipation can lead to increased interest and engagement with your brand.
2. **Building a qualified lead list:** A waitlist allows businesses to capture the contact information of interested prospects. These prospects have already shown a level of interest in your product or service, making

them more likely to convert into paying customers.

3. **Gaining market insights:** Through the waitlist process, businesses can gather valuable data and insights about their target audience. This information can be used to refine marketing strategies, tailor product offerings, and improve overall customer experience.
4. **Creating social proof:** A waitlist can help create social proof by showcasing the demand for your product or service. When potential customers see others eagerly signing up for the waitlist, it can increase their trust and confidence in your brand.

How to Implement a Waitlist Strategy with ScoreApp

ScoreApp can be a valuable tool for implementing a waitlist strategy effectively. Here's how:

1. **Capture leads:** ScoreApp allows businesses to create customized waitlist landing pages where potential customers

can sign up and provide their contact information. This ensures that businesses can capture leads efficiently and build a qualified list of interested prospects.
2. **Automated email communication:** ScoreApp enables businesses to set up automated email sequences to nurture and engage with waitlist subscribers. This helps maintain their interest, provide updates, and build a relationship with potential customers.
3. **Segmentation and personalization:** ScoreApp offers segmentation capabilities, allowing businesses to categorize waitlist subscribers based on their preferences or interests. This segmentation enables personalized communication, ensuring that subscribers receive relevant information tailored to their needs.
4. **Analytics and reporting:** ScoreApp provides analytics and reporting features that allow businesses to track the performance of their waitlist campaigns. This data helps in optimizing the strategy,

identifying areas for improvement, and measuring the success of the lead generation efforts.

Successful Companies Using Waitlist Strategy

Several successful companies have effectively utilized waitlist strategies to generate leads and create buzz around their products or services. Here are a few examples:

1. **Clubhouse:** Clubhouse, a social networking app, initially launched with an invite-only waitlist strategy. This exclusivity created a sense of curiosity and demand, leading to a surge in interest and user sign-ups.
2. **Tesla:** Tesla, the electric vehicle manufacturer, has used waitlists to generate leads for their new vehicle releases. By allowing customers to reserve their spot in line and providing regular updates, Tesla has been able to build excitement and convert waitlist subscribers into customers.
3. **Dropbox:** Dropbox, a cloud storage service, famously used a waitlist strategy during its

early days. By offering additional storage space to users who referred friends to join the waitlist, Dropbox was able to rapidly grow its user base and generate leads.

These examples demonstrate how companies have successfully leveraged waitlist strategies to generate leads, create demand, and build a loyal customer base.

A waitlist strategy can be an effective way to generate leads by creating anticipation, building a qualified lead list, gaining market insights, and creating social proof. **ScoreApp** provides the necessary tools and features to implement a waitlist strategy efficiently, allowing businesses to capture leads, automate communication, personalize messaging, and track performance. By leveraging the power of a waitlist strategy, businesses can generate interest, build anticipation, and convert leads into loyal customers.

This also increases the demand and supply tension, when your potential customers see the competition, and how many people sign up for your waitlist it moves them to take quick action when the product is ready. Companies like Apple, Tesla, Rolex, amongst others use this strategy to sell out within hours after product launch.

Let's use Rolex as an example to illustrate the effectiveness of their waitlist strategy. Imagine that after Rolex launches a new collection, they receive an overwhelming response with approximately 1 million potential customers expressing their desire to purchase the original Rolex. However, Rolex only has 700,000 Rolexes available for sale.

To manage this high demand, Rolex implements a waitlist system. They promptly reach out to all those who signed up for the waitlist via email. In their communication, Rolex explains that they can reserve a watch for each customer for a limited period of 3 days. If the customer doesn't complete the purchase within this timeframe, the watch will be made available to another customer.

For those unable to secure a watch from the initial batch, Rolex informs them that they will have to wait for another 18 months (about 1 and a half years), to have the opportunity to purchase a genuine Rolex. This ensures a sense of exclusivity and anticipation for the customers on the waitlist, as they eagerly await their turn to acquire one of these prestigious timepieces. Additionally, joining the waitlist again becomes necessary to maintain their position in the queue.

Rolex effectively creates a sense of scarcity and exclusivity around their products. This not only generates buzz and excitement but also cultivates a strong desire among potential customers to own a Rolex watch. This approach is not only utilized by Rolex but also by various other companies seeking to drive demand and maintain their brand's exclusivity.

ONLINE DISCUSSION GROUPS

Our third low cost but effective lead generation strategy is creating an online discussion group. This is indeed a powerful strategy for generating hot leads.

These are virtual communities where individuals with shared interests can engage in conversations, share insights, and support one another. For businesses, these platforms offer a unique opportunity to connect with potential customers in a more personal and interactive way.

Why Use Online Discussion Groups?

1. **Community Building:** By building a community around your product or service, you create an environment where members feel a sense of belonging and investment in your brand.

2. **Engagement:** Regular discussions keep your audience engaged and interested in what you have to offer. This consistent engagement builds trust and positions your

business as a thought leader in your industry.

3. **Feedback Loop:** These groups serve as a direct line to your customer base, allowing you to gather feedback, understand pain points, and tailor your offerings to meet their needs.

4. **Soft Selling:** Instead of hard selling, discussion groups allow you to softly introduce your products or services within the context of relevant conversations, making the sales process feel more organic and less intrusive.

How to Maximize the Potential of Online Discussion Groups

- **Identify the Right Platforms:** Choose platforms where your target audience is most active. LinkedIn is ideal for B2B products, while Facebook and WhatsApp might be better suited for B2C interactions. The good thing about all these platforms is that you can create an account for free, and create a discussion group within it, and it's also free.

- **Create Valuable Content:** Share content that is informative, helpful, and relevant to the group's interests. This could include how-to guides, industry news, or case studies demonstrating the effectiveness of your product.

- **Encourage Participation:** Pose questions, create polls, and initiate discussions that encourage members to participate. The more active the group, the more opportunities you must showcase your expertise and the benefits of your product.

- **Offer Exclusive Benefits:** Provide group members with exclusive offers, early access to new products, or special discounts. This not only incentivizes participation but also drives sales.

- **Monitor and Respond:** Be active in the group and respond promptly to questions and comments. This shows that you value the community and that you are committed to providing support.

- **Leverage User-Generated Content:** Encourage members to share their own experiences with your product. Positive testimonials from peers can be incredibly persuasive.

- **Host Live Events:** Organize webinars, Q&A sessions, or live demonstrations to deepen engagement and provide real-time interaction with your audience.

Let me talk more on Hosting live events. Hosting webinars and live streams has become a pivotal strategy for businesses looking to enhance lead generation. These virtual gatherings offer a multitude of benefits that traditional methods may lack.

For instance, they provide a platform for real-time interaction, building deeper connections and a more memorable brand experience for attendees. This direct engagement is useful for capturing attention and nurturing leads.

Moreover, online events are accessible to a global audience, breaking geographical barriers and expanding the potential customer base. They are also more cost-effective, eliminating the need for physical venues and travel, which can be a significant financial burden. This cost reduction doesn't come at the expense of reach; in fact, it allows for scalability without proportional increases in expense.

One of the most compelling advantages of virtual events is the wealth of data they provide. You can track attendee behavior, measure engagement, and collect real-time feedback. This data is crucial for refining marketing strategies and understanding what resonates with your audience.

In terms of metrics, surveys have shown that most businesses find virtual events to be effective for lead generation. It's essential to track success through various indicators, such as ticket sales, attendee feedback, and engagement with follow-up campaigns. These metrics offer insights into the effectiveness of the event and guide future improvements.

I want you to really let into these strategies within your online discussion groups, you can warm up your audience, showcase the value of your offerings, and ultimately convert engaged members into hot leads.

Have in mind, the key is to provide genuine value and build a community that supports and uplifts its members. This approach not only generates leads but also cultivates loyal customers who are more likely to advocate for your brand.

WORKSHOPS/SEMINARS

Hosting workshops or seminars is a fantastic strategy for generating hot leads, especially when it is small and focused. These types of workshops or seminars offer a more intimate setting, which is conducive to deeper discussions and personal interactions. This environment allows for a level of engagement that larger events cannot match. It is more ideal if you're into B2B because it requires a small group of people with lots of money, it's my favorite.

Benefits of Small Workshops/Seminars

1. **Personal Interaction:** Smaller events facilitate face-to-face conversations, allowing for immediate feedback and the opportunity to address specific questions or concerns about your product or service.

2. **Focused Attention:** With fewer participants, each one gets more attention, making them feel valued and heard. This can lead to stronger relationships and a higher likelihood of conversion.

3. **Cost-Effective:** Hosting smaller events is generally more budget-friendly than large-

scale seminars, making it an accessible option for small businesses looking to generate leads without breaking the bank.

4. **Flexibility:** Smaller workshops can be more easily adapted to the needs and interests of the attendees, creating a tailored experience that resonates with them.

5. **Community Building:** These events can help build a community of loyal customers who are more likely to refer others to your business.

Step-by-Step Guide on How to Effectively Invite Your B2B Prospects

Step 1: Identify Your Target Audience

Before sending out invitations, clearly define who your target audience is. Consider the types of businesses that would benefit from your workshop and the roles within those businesses that are decision-makers or influencers.

Step 2: Create a Compelling Invitation

Create an invitation that highlights the value of attending your workshop. Emphasize the benefits, the problems it will solve, and the unique opportunities for learning and networking that attendees will experience.

Step 3: Personalize Your Invitations

Personalization can significantly increase the chances of your invitation being accepted. Address the prospects by name, reference their company, and mention how the workshop is relevant to their specific business challenges.

Step 4: Utilize Multiple Channels

Reach out to your prospects through various channels. This can include:

- **Email Marketing:** Send personalized emails with a clear call-to-action.

- **Social Media:** Use platforms like LinkedIn to connect with prospects and send direct messages.

- **Phone Calls:** Follow up with a phone call to add a personal touch and answer any questions.

- **Partnerships:** Collaborate with industry partners who can help promote your event to their audience.

Step 5: Provide Clear Details

Ensure that your invitation includes all the necessary details such as the date, time, location (or link, if online), agenda, and speakers. Make it easy for prospects to RSVP (Reply/Response) or learn more about the event.

Step 6: Follow-Up

Send reminders as the event approaches and follow up with prospects who haven't responded. A gentle nudge can often convert a maybe into a yes.

Step 7: Offer Incentives

Consider offering early bird discounts, exclusive content, or other incentives to encourage prospects to sign up.

Step 8: Track and Analyze Responses

Monitor the responses to your invitations and analyze the data to refine your approach for future events.

By following these steps and leveraging the insights from your research, you can effectively invite your B2B prospects to workshops and seminars, creating valuable opportunities for lead generation and business growth.

Maximizing the Impact of Your Workshops/Seminars

Targeted Content: Ensure the content of your workshop or seminar is highly relevant to the attendees. This could involve addressing common pain points, showcasing the benefits of your product, or providing actionable advice.

- **Interactive Format:** Design the event to be interactive, encouraging participants to engage in discussions, share their experiences, and provide input on your offerings.

- **Follow-Up:** After the event, follow up with attendees to thank them for their participation, provide additional resources, and gently guide them towards your product or service.

- **Leverage Testimonials:** Use positive feedback from workshop participants as testimonials to attract future leads.

- **Continuous Improvement:** Gather feedback from each event to improve future workshops and ensure they remain effective in lead generation.

If you want to focus on the quality of interactions rather than the quantity of attendees, small workshops and seminars can be a powerful tool in your lead generation arsenal. These types of events provide a platform for demonstrating expertise, building trust, and ultimately, converting attendees into hot leads.

PRIVATE DINNER

The last but not the least strategy on our list is organizing private dinner events. This is an excellent strategy for lead generation, combining the personal touch of face-to-face interaction with the exclusivity of a select gathering.

Inviting industry experts to a private dinner doesn't have to be expensive. These are some low-cost strategies to make it feasible:

1. **Host Small, Intimate Dinners:** Instead of renting out a large venue, focus on creating an intimate setting. A dinner table for 12 people is perfect. Smaller gatherings allow for more meaningful conversations and personal connections.

2. **Choose Budget-Friendly Locations:** Look for affordable venues or even consider hosting the dinner at your own home. A cozy atmosphere can be just as effective as an upscale restaurant.

3. **Collaborate with Partners:** Reach out to industry partners or complementary businesses. They might be willing to co-host the dinner or contribute to the costs. In

return, you can offer them exposure to your network.

4. **Potluck Style:** Consider a potluck-style dinner where each guest brings a dish. This not only reduces costs but also adds a communal feel to the event.

5. **Focus on Value:** The goal is to provide value to your guests. Instead of expensive gourmet meals, prioritize quality ingredients and thoughtful preparation. Remember, it's about the experience and connections, not just the food.

6. **Use Local Ingredients:** Support local farmers and suppliers by using seasonal and locally sourced ingredients. Not only is this cost-effective, but it also aligns with sustainability and community-building.

7. **DIY Decor:** Keep decorations simple. Candles, fresh flowers, and personalized place cards can create an elegant ambiance without breaking the bank.

8. **Leverage Social Media:** Document the dinner and share highlights on social media. This not only extends the reach of your

event but also showcases your brand's personality.

Hosting a private dinner party is like organizing a small seminar or workshop as we've discussed in our previous strategy, but with a more relaxed and social atmosphere. This setting allows for deeper, more meaningful conversations and can lead to stronger business relationships.

Key Elements of a Successful Private Dinner Event

1. **Exclusivity:** The allure of exclusivity cannot be overstated. Inviting a selected group of top prospects and industry experts can help you create a sense of importance and urgency that can pique interest and encourage attendance.

2. **Networking Opportunities:** A small dinner setting is perfect for networking. Guests can interact with each other in a more personal way, which can lead to collaborations, partnerships, and referrals.

3. **Product Introduction:** Use this opportunity to introduce your product or service in a subtle, non-salesy manner. Focus on how it

can solve problems or add value to the guests' businesses.

4. **Tapping into Other People's Networks:** By inviting industry experts, you're not just reaching the guests at the table; you're tapping into their wider networks. A positive impression can lead to word-of-mouth referrals and expanded reach.

5. **Feedback Collection:** In such an intimate setting, you can gather honest feedback about your offerings, which can be invaluable for future improvements and marketing strategies.

Enhancing the Private Dinner Experience

Enhancing the private dinner experience involves thoughtful planning and execution. Let's talk about it in more details:

Personalized Invitations

You must create invitations that make each guest feel special and valued. Address them by name, mention their industry expertise, and highlight the other notable attendees. Personalization creates anticipation and sets a positive tone for the event.

For instance, you might write:

"Dear [Guest's Name],

We are delighted to invite you to an exclusive private dinner on [Date] at [Venue]. As an industry leader in [Guest's Industry], your insights are invaluable. Join us for an evening of engaging conversations with fellow experts, including [Other Notable Attendees]. Your presence will enrich our discussions on [Themed Topic]. We look forward to sharing a delightful meal and building meaningful connections.

Kindly RSVP by [RSVP Deadline]. We appreciate your contribution to our community.

Warm regards,

[Your Name]"

Themed Discussions

Plan the evening around a relevant theme. Whether it's related to your industry, a specific business challenge, or a trending topic, themed discussions serve as conversation starters. They keep the dialogue focused and engaging. For example:

"Our theme for the evening is 'Innovation in Digital Marketing.' As we gather around the table, we'll explore strategies for leveraging emerging technologies to enhance customer engagement.

Each guest will have the opportunity to share their experiences and insights. We'll discuss topics such as AI-driven personalization, data analytics, and omnichannel marketing. Prepare to be inspired and contribute to our collective knowledge."

Incorporating these elements creates an unforgettable private dinner experience—one that not only delights your guests but also contributes to your lead generation efforts. It's about more than just the food; it's about building meaningful connections in a relaxed and intimate setting. Bear in mind, relationships built over a meal can lead to long-lasting business collaborations and referrals.

After the event, follow up with a personalized thank you note and any promised resources or information. This keeps the conversation going and reinforces the relationship. Collect feedback from attendees to measure the success of the event and learn how to improve future dinners.

Remember, the magic of private dinners lies in the personal connections you make. Even on a budget, you can create a memorable experience that leaves a lasting impression on your guests and generates warm leads for your business.

Hosting private dinner parties does not just generate leads; it creates advocates for your brand. The personal connections made during these events can lead to long-term business relationships and ongoing lead generation opportunities. The goal is to provide a memorable experience that showcases the value of your product or service, all while enjoying good food and great company.

SUMMARY

We've demystified the top 5 lead generation strategies used by business giants. We've revealed that the key to exponential growth lies not in the size of the marketing budget but in the strategic lead generation and thoughtful engagement with potential customers.

In conclusion, we've demystified the top 5 lead generation strategies used by business giants. We've revealed that the key to exponential growth lies not in the size of the marketing budget but in the strategic lead generation and thoughtful engagement with potential customers.

Small businesses have the potential to rival industry titans by implementing the same lead generation strategies that have long been kept secret. By focusing on the customer's needs and creating a sense of urgency through limited availability, businesses can transform their lead generation process and experience unprecedented success.

The five strategies outlined serve as a blueprint for creating a robust pipeline of leads, ensuring that businesses are not just surviving, but thriving. With these tools, small business owners are equipped to step out of the shadows of complacency and into the spotlight of remarkable achievement.

Embrace these strategies, and watch as your business transcends the ordinary, becoming a beacon of innovation and prosperity in the marketplace. This strategy will help you unlock the full potential of your business and set a new standard for success.

RECOMMENDATIONS

I highly recommend you use **ScoreApp** for your lead generation, especially for most of the strategies we've discussed in this book. This is an advanced quiz funnel marketing tool that allows businesses to create and optimize their entire quiz marketing funnel within one platform. It is designed to make it as easy as possible to set up and start generating high-quality leads quickly. **Click here** now to get started for free or **Get 50% off your first month** subscription automatically.

I also recommend you watch this podcast. Here you will see how some of the strategies I've discussed in this book are analyzed and implemented in real-time by Daniel Priestly the founder of ScoreApp. If you have the hardcopy of this book, you can check on "**New Way to Get Clients on Demand: Complete Blueprint w/ Daniel Priestley**" on **The Futur** YouTube channel.

www.ingramcontent.com/pod-product-compliance
Lightning Source LLC
Chambersburg PA
CBHW070946220526
45471CB00007B/2919